Road Blocks

by

Colonel G. A. Wade

ROYAL ARMOURIES

First published by Gale & Polden, *c.*1942
This edition published by Royal Armouries Museum,
Armouries Drive, Leeds LS10 1LT, United Kingdom
www.royalarmouries.org

© 2024 Trustees of the Royal Armouries

All rights reserved. No part of this publication may be reproduced,
stored in a retrieval system or transmitted in any form or by any means,
electronic, mechanical, photocopying, recording or otherwise
without the prior permission of the publisher.

ISBN 978 1 913013 48 6

A CIP record for this book is available from the British Library

Every effort has been made to contact copyright holders.
Royal Armouries will be happy to correct any errors or omissions
brought to their attention.

Typesetting by Typo•glyphix

10 9 8 7 6 5 4 3 2 1

The original version of *Road Blocks* contained some full colour diagrams,
which have been reproduced here in greyscale.
Mention of colour in the text has been retained for accuracy.

ROAD BLOCKS

BY
COLONEL G.A. WADE, M.C.
Author of "The Defence of Bloodford Village" etc.

SUMMARY

IMPORTANCE OF ROAD BLOCKS.
    Casual obstructions—nuisance—bore.
    Tiny battlefield.
    Ebb and flow of fighting.
    Symbolic—gesture of **defiance.**
    " Beyond this you shall not come! "

THREE CLASSIFICATIONS.
    Major—minor—mobile obstacles.
    Major blocks will vary as enemy tanks alter.

SITE FOR DEFENCE.
    Fit in with general scheme of defence.
    " Where you site, there you will fight! "
    Make difficult to attack—easy to defend.
    Front—flanks—rear.
    Unexpectedness—three situations (Plate).
    Round a corner—reverse of rise—sudden dip.
    Defiles, deep ditches, thick woods, cuttings.

USE OF SCREENS.
    Protects block from gun fire—wastes ammunition.
    Uncertainty of invaders' supplies.

DEFENDERS.
    Must completely control block and approaches.
    Guard flanks and rear.
    Alternative positions to move to.

LIE DOGGO—HIT HARD—CLEAR OUT.
    Repeat the formula.
    Enemy never knows where you are.
    Implies number of positions known or prepared.

ILLUSTRATION DOGGO-HIT-QUIT TACTICS.
>Describe action.
>Arrival of scouts of fighting patrol.
>"To see what all the row was about."
>German mortar team.
>Staff officer—"Extraordinary, no casualties."
>"No reason why we **should** have."
>**A great truth.**

ACTIVE DEFENCE OF ROAD BLOCKS.
>Careful, final siting.
>"What's wrong with the ruddy thing?"
>Too close to wood—or Houses dominate defenders—or "Tank can go round it."
>"Barbed wire," "Occupying houses," "Anti-tank mines."

HOW WILL HUN ATTACK?
>"Bloodlust and swank."
>Creeping Boches.

"YOU ATTACK MY ROAD BLOCK AND I'LL ATTACK YOU!"
>No easy reconnaissance.
>Get your blow in first!

THE FIGHT AT CYMROS.
>Describe it.

GENERAL OBSERVATIONS.
>Road blocks in **depth.**
>Not enough men.
>Depth on **some** roads.

EIGHT MISTAKES IN SITING.
>Detail them.

HALTING TRAFFIC.
>Do not allow unexamined vehicles to approach.
>Light obstacle 150 yards away.

TREES.
>Difficult to remove.
>Look-outs and fire bombers.

(R.BL.)

CAMOUFLAGE.
> Your life may depend on it.
> Tracks.
> Put something he **can** spot.
> Hun shooting not accurate.

BLUFF.
> Blocking four streets in a hurry.
> Carpets—bricks—humps.
> "One Hun less!"
> Dummy for dive-bombing.

OTHER WEAPONS.
> Hoses throwing water or live steam.
> Electrical entanglements.
> Refugees—trailer pump.

FIGHTING PATROLS.
> Look-outs signal to patrol.
> Frequently happens one block attacked—Twenty doing nothing.

TRAPS.
> Scope for ingenuity.
> Give confidence to defence.
> "Try your hand; you may have a flair!"

ROUTINE.
> May man blocks a long time.
> Orders to **Road Block Commander.**
> Orders for **guards on road blocks.**
> Conscientious N.C.O. required—hard work.
> Fair spells of duty.
> Posting roster up.
> Aim to keep men fresh and fit, not "bitched, b——d and bewildered."
> Routine matters most important.

EXTRAORDINARILY INTERESTING SUBJECT.
> Imparted my enthusiasm.

"REASON OUT THE WHY AND WHEREFORE FOR YOURSELF."

ROAD BLOCKS

IMPORTANCE OF ROAD BLOCKS

I DOUBT if there can be found in the whole of soldierly activities a more interesting subject than road blocks; and yet, by most people, they appear to be regarded merely as casual obstructions in the road, a *nuisance* to traffic, and a *bore* to defend.

The reason I find them so interesting is that, whenever I see a road block I say to myself, "Here is a tiny battlefield. Here men may one day encounter each other in deadly combat. Here, in miniature, all the great principles of strategy and tactics will apply just as much as when whole armies join issue," and my imagination at once begins to picture the ebb and flow of fighting for possession of the road block, with every little detail of the surroundings acquiring a sinister significance. A road block to all soldiers should be symbolic. A road block is a challenge thrown down by free men to Hitler and his hordes—a gesture of DEFIANCE which says, "Beyond this you shall not come!"

Although at the present moment the road block looks out of place in its peaceful surroundings, who knows what it will be in a few months' time? It may be all that separates freedom from armoured tyranny; it may be the one obstacle which, desperately held, will affect the course of a mighty battle.

Once you get this point of view—and it is the ONLY common-sense way of looking at road blocks—you will be prepared to give a great deal of time and study to their siting, construction and defence.

Road blocks may be divided into three classifications —major road blocks, capable of stopping tanks; minor road blocks, which a tank could cross but not an armoured car or other vehicle; and mobile obstacles, such as carts, wagons and old motor-cars which can be used quickly in emergency to form some sort of hindrance to the enemy.

Major road blocks will be used solely to close roads through tank obstacles, as it would obviously be absurd to place a huge, expensive road block on a road which has open country round it which a tank could, if it was diverted from the road, traverse easily. Incidentally, the form and arrangement of major road blocks will vary from time to time to meet the changes in the performance of enemy armoured fighting vehicles.

SITE YOUR ROAD BLOCKS FOR DEFENCE

The siting of road blocks is bound up very closely with the general scheme of defence. If a town, village or locality is to be defended, obviously the enemy must be denied use of the roads running into the place.

Now you may take it as an axiom that where you place your road block *there* you will have to FIGHT; so you should site it with the idea of placing an attacking enemy as much at a disadvantage as possible; in other words, put it where it is DIFFICULT TO ATTACK and EASY TO DEFEND.

If you always assume that your road block will be heavily attacked from front, flanks and rear, you will some day have great cause for thankfulness and self-congratulation.

It is very good tactics to site the block where the enemy will come upon it unexpectedly, causing him to hesitate on exactly the spot where you have everything prepared to take full advantage of his temporary embarrassment.

To effect this there are three situations in which blocks may be put: round a corner, on the reverse side of a rise in the road, such as is occasioned by a humpbacked bridge, or tucked away in a sudden dip in the road.

Defiles, deep ditches, thick woods and cuttings are all features helping to make road blocks effective, so make all possible use of them.

GOOD SITES FOR ROAD BLOCKS

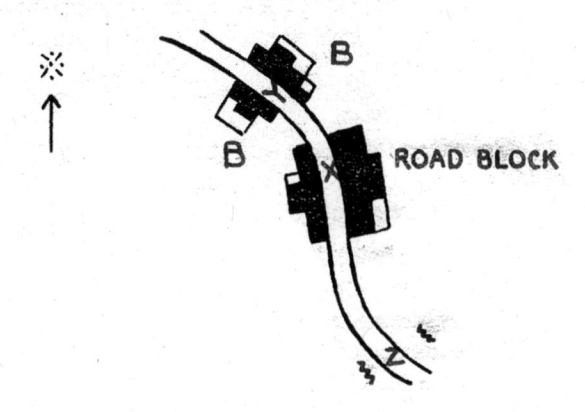

At a Bend in the Road

This block is defended in both directions. Vehicles from NORTH would first see road block and stop at Y.

Bombers B are in houses on both sides ready to perform as soon as vehicle stops.

From SOUTH traffic would halt about Z. No houses here, so bombers are in slit trenches.

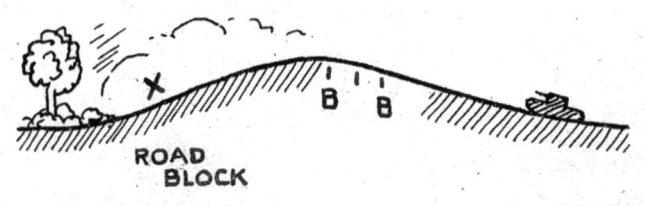

Beyond a Crest

The climbing vehicle cannot see the obstacle till the crest is reached.

Molotov throwers should be stationed about BB.

ROAD
BLOCK

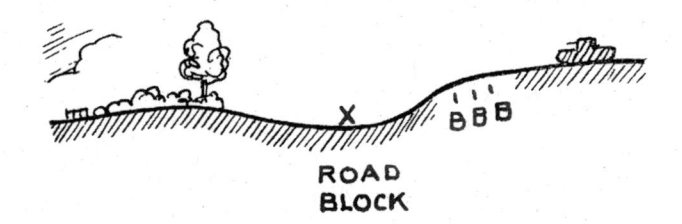

In an Unexpected Dip

Sometimes there is a dip in the road and it is not noticeable, because the road carries straight on beyond it.

This is a good place to surprise a fast-moving vehicle.

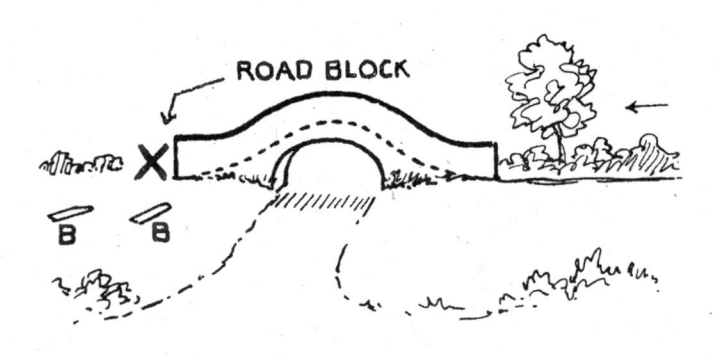

ROAD BLOCK

On a Hump-backed Bridge

Usually found over canals, these make first-rate road blocks.

The block itself must be robust and fastened to bridge if possible.

Bombers are in well-camouflaged slit trenches at BB.

It may not be possible to take advantage of any of these surprise positions, and the road block, to fit in with other defensive arrangements, may have to be so placed that it is in full view of the approaching enemy for a considerable distance. If the enemy happen to be in a tank, they will at once shoot at the block to demolish it sufficiently to make it passable. To obviate this it is wise to screen it with hessian or carpets, blankets, sheets, etc., taken from nearby houses. A screen of this kind will take a lot of punishment and still remain a screen.

Never forget that when the Germans invade us their future supplies will be uncertain in the extreme, so that every round we can induce them to expend ineffectively is one less for them to fight with.

The next thing to consider in siting the road block is where you will place its defenders so that they have complete control of the block and the approaches to it and yet cannot be outflanked or taken in the rear.

Sometimes the alteration of the site by only a few yards will be enough to enable more weapons of various kinds to be brought to bear on it, and the road leading to it, from other positions behind or on one side.

If you are hard put to it to defend a road block, reinforcements may be sent to help you, and these will need positions to occupy.

In addition, every man defending the block should have several alternative positions to move to after firing.

The whole idea of the defenders should be to hold their fire till the range is so short that it will have devastating effect. *Then,* having delivered their blow at the enemy, to dodge away into some other concealed position to watch the place they have just left being

" strafed," and to be ready with another telling burst of fire when the Germans advance again in the belief that they have effectively scuppered the British who fired before.

The action of the road-block garrison in defence should be: LIE DOGGO—HIT STRAIGHT AND HARD—CLEAR OUT STEALTHILY to new position —LIE DOGGO—HIT AGAIN—QUIT AGAIN— DOGGO AGAIN.

By doing this the enemy never knows where you are and you are observing what I think is a *cardinal point* in war: having hit the enemy you do not wait where he knows you are, to see what he does about it.

But all this implies a number of positions already known and, where necessary, prepared; so you must bear this in mind when siting the road block (or what might better be described as the STORM CENTRE).

Here is an illustration of what I mean by DOGGO— HIT—QUIT tactics (see Plate on next page):—

Before the enemy arrived the defenders were disposed in HOUSE A and slit trenches at 1. Two German motor-cyclists came along from the north-east, saw the road block and were about to go back when an enemy tank came round the bend at great speed and stopped at Z.

A.W. bombs and Molotovs were immediately flung on to it from 1, but unfortunately the tank reversed so quickly that it was out of range before sufficient bombs to more than warm up and alarm the crew had hit it. The tank retired to cover of WOOD at Y, and the motor-cyclists opened tommy-gun fire on slit trench at 1.

This was more than the defenders at A could stand and they opened fire, killing one motor-cyclist and wounding the other, who dashed off after the tank.

14

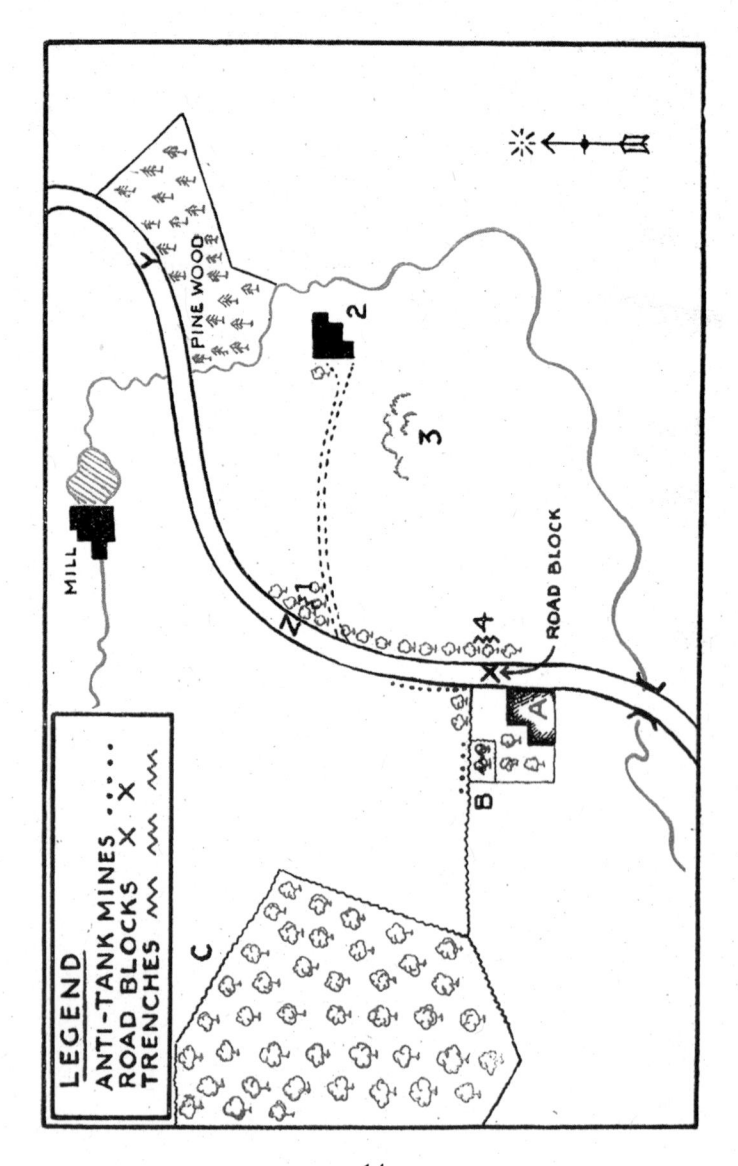

Defenders from 1 moved to HOUSE 2, and men from A moved to weapon pits at B.

Soon afterwards the enemy carried two trench mortars down the stream to behind the MILL, and as they opened fire on HOUSE A a machine gun from edge of PINEWOOD fired heavily on slit trenches at 1.

After two hits had been scored on the house two parties of Germans emerged from the wood, one proceeding south-west to attack the slit trenches and the other coming up the stream apparently with the idea of working round house at A.

Defenders in HOUSE 2 held their fire until the last moment and then downed eight of the Germans before the remainder escaped back to the wood.

On hearing the firing the officer leading the Germans against the slit trenches wheeled them round and dashed towards HOUSE 2 obviously hoping to take the defenders there in the flank while they were engaged with the other party.

This manœuvre was seen by the defenders at B, who opened fire so effectively that this party retreated after the other, leaving several grey heaps writhing on the field.

Defenders from 2 then moved back to patch of shrub at 3, and those from B crept along hedge to WOOD at C.

The mortars got busy again, one on to B and the other on to HOUSE 2. A lot of ammunition was expended before hits were obtained, but as soon as this had been done enemy came out of PINEWOOD again and advanced quickly. Unfortunately, an excitable man opened fire too soon from 3 and the Germans went back again. A few minutes later both mortars started throwing up the earth round the bushes at 3, but by this time the men from there, knowing their position had been given away, were tucked away in the slit trenches at 4, moistening the wicks of the Molotovs and getting things ready there.

Soon afterwards the enemy changed their tactics and the tank came round the bend charging up to the road block, firing as it came.

It almost mounted the block, then got itself bellied and swayed and twisted for a few seconds helplessly. That was long enough! First one flaming bottle and then another came hurtling from the security of the slit trenches at 4 till the tank was a roaring inferno and black clouds rose up into the sky. Soon its engines misfired and stopped. There the awe-inspiring tank was—nothing but a ghastly ruin!

Seeing the fate of the tank the German infantry who had followed it hesitated and stopped, forming a splendid target for the defenders at C, who started flattening them at easy range.

This was the situation when the forward scouts of one of our fighting patrols arrived from the south to see what all the row was about.

In a few minutes the patrol had moved down the stream and was mopping up the remains of the German infantry in PINEWOOD. What happened to the German mortar team was interesting: apparently when the defenders moved from B to C and looked out towards the Mill they could see the Huns operating the mortars in full view, but as they were doing no harm—in fact, were wasting their ammunition—the Corporal refrained from opening fire.

Soon after the tank had conked out the mortar team started to pack up and withdraw to Y. That was the time to let them have it! Only two men succeeded in crossing the space between the Mill and Pinewood, and that did not matter much, as they met our fighting patrol just coming out!

Later on, when things had quietened down, a number of Staff officers were having the fight reconstructed for them. One said, " You have captured a tank, killed seventeen Germans, wounded and captured a lot of others—a SPLENDID PERFORMANCE; but what is so extraordinary is that you have not had a single casualty amongst your own men!" To which the Sergeant replied, "Well, sir, there was NO REASON WHY WE *SHOULD* HAVE ANY CASUALTIES."

At that, silence fell on the little group. The Sergeant had uttered a GREAT TRUTH!

As a matter of fact, the defenders did have a casualty. The man who fired the premature shot from the bushes at 3 had lost two teeth and the skin of his nose. No one quite knew how, but the Sergeant looked acutely embarrassed when it was mentioned.

The only man who was disappointed in this smart action was the A/T mine artist, who had put his mines on the west of the road in the hope that the tank would veer that way on seeing the block. He will probably have better luck next time.

Now you will have noted that the defenders would have had very serious casualties if they had not kept quiet till they hit with all their might and then moved AT ONCE—what I call DOGGO—HIT—QUIT tactics.

But they had to have their various positions and plans prepared beforehand and the road block had to be sited in a locality suitable for the tactics to be employed.

So much for the siting of road blocks; now for their defence.

ACTIVE DEFENCE OF ROAD BLOCKS

Having to site your road block so that it conforms to the general scheme of defence imposes serious limitations upon your choice of position, but I will assume that you have, with due regard to the main defence on the one hand and the surrounding tactical features on the other, selected your spot. Then ask yourself, " Would it be better a little farther up the road or a wee bit down? "

When it is absolutely fixed you will probably be dissatisfied, because it is very, very seldom that one can get a perfectly sited road block, so ask yourself, " Why am I dissatisfied with this position? " (or, being you, you will more probably say to yourself, " What's wrong with the ruddy thing? ").

Your answer to this question will have a far-reaching effect upon your defensive dispositions.

You may say, " It is too close to the corner of the wood and the enemy could sneak up under cover," or, " The houses over there dominate the defenders' positions," or, " A tank can go round it," and immediately you begin thinking in terms of barbed wire, occupying houses, or placing anti-tank mines.

After that go down the road, out of sight of the selected position, puff yourself up with bloodlust and swank, and approach the road block imagining that you are a Nazi invader.

Picture how the Hun will attack. Visualize the creeping Boches looking for the defenders and planning to get to close quarters with them. After that you will find that your defensive dispositions will come easily to your mind.

Whilst on this subject of defence, do not make the fashionable blunder of considering only STATIC defence, but say, "You attack my road block and I'll attack YOU!"

Make up your mind that any enemy temporarily halted is NOT going to be allowed comfortably to reconnoitre the position, calmly study your defences and peacefully devise a plan to land the whole lot of you into the hereafter.

Consider how you will harass and hinder his preparations and deployment; in fact, if you are half a chap you will consider how you can GET YOUR BLOW IN *FIRST*!

This attitude of mind is brought out vividly in the case of the road block at CYMROS.

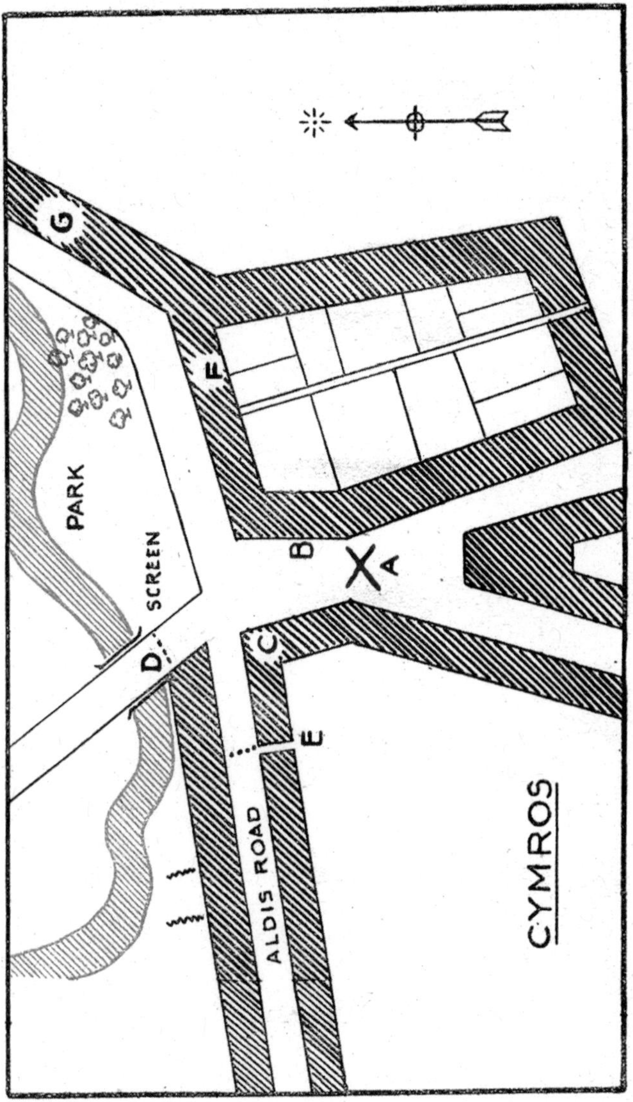
G
F
PARK
SCREEN
B
X
A
C
D
E
ALDIS ROAD
CYMROS

THE FIGHT AT CYMROS

The retreating British forces, having decided to hold this town, put a road block at A which they intended to defend from the houses at B and C. They also threw a screen across the road at D and had two men with anti-tank mines on a board concealed in an entry at E.

Look-outs reported two tanks approaching from the north-east preceded by motor-cyclists and followed by three lorry loads of infantry. The cyclists came round the corner, saw the road block, swerved to one side and proceeded along ALDIS ROAD.

When they had passed, the two men concealed in the entry heard the tanks approaching and pushed out the mines in front of the leading one, blowing off its tracks and completely blocking the street.

The second tank stopped, looked at the screen over the bridge, hesitated a moment, and then charged the road block at A; only to be greeted by showers of blazing bottles from which it was just escaping when its engine drew in flame instead of air and stopped. The crew got out and would have surrendered, but a defender with a tommy-gun apparently misunderstood their intention.

After this the Platoon Commander (who was in the house C) said, "What will those infantry do now?" The Sergeant replied, "I'll bet they'll start mortaring us like blazes and then attack for all they are worth, sir."

"Where do you think they will put the mortars, Sergeant?"

"Behind them there trees in the park, sir."

"Right," said the Platoon Commander. "Get your men out of here before they start."

"Where shall we go to, sir?" asked the Sergeant.

"Behind 'them there trees' in the park and we will bring the mortars back with us!" said the officer.

How very true is the saying "Fortune favours the brave"! Leaving a small guard on the road block and sending an L.M.G. team to occupy house at F, the

Platoon Commander led his men through the houses, yards and entries to the building at G. Peeping through the window, he saw the three lorries under the trees at the other side of the road. They were empty, but he could see the backs of the Boches moving amongst the bushes in the park, and saw a mortar bomb sail up into the air and sweep towards the building at C. All the Germans seemed very intent upon this attack.

Leaving picked marksmen at G, he took his men swiftly and silently across the road behind the lorries, scuppered three drivers and was charging the backs of the astonished Germans before they could turn round.

It was not even a fight. Those who ran north were easy meat for men at G. Those who ran south were machine-gunned from F.

The last thing in the world the enemy had expected was to be attacked suddenly from the rear. There is a lesson in that.

Here are a few general observations which you may find helpful:—

ROAD BLOCKS IN DEPTH

The ideal arrangement of road blocks is in DEPTH, so that, if an enemy vehicle succeeds in passing one, he soon bumps up against another.

Usually, to obtain depth all round a town or village so many road blocks would be necessary that there would not be sufficient men to guard them. By using a little cunning, however, it is possible to arrange a certain depth on the roads most likely to be used by the enemy.

Watch this point when siting your road blocks in the first place.

Eight Mistakes in Siting Road Blocks

1. Using two blocks where one will do.

2. Leaving an entry, as shown by dotted line.

3. Block in indefensible position when houses are available to defend it from.

4. Block out in "the blue," forming no part of general defence scheme.

5. Block on straight road; should be round the bend.

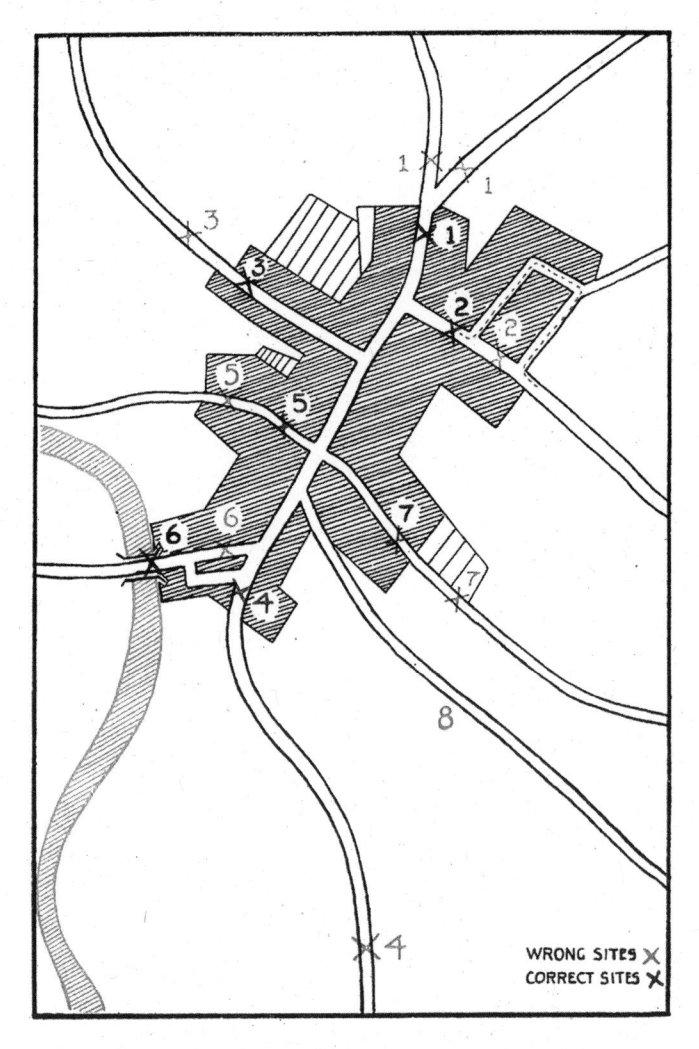

6. Block not denying the bridge to the enemy.
7. Block sited where tank can get round.
8. Road overlooked altogether.

HALTING TRAFFIC AT A DISTANCE

When an enemy may be in the vicinity it is all wrong to allow an unexamined vehicle to approach right up to the road block before it is halted.

Suppose that, suddenly, from a harmless-looking van jumped half a dozen men firing tommy-guns or automatic pistols, what chance would the guard have? Not an earthly!

The only way to obviate surprise attack of this kind is to have a light obstacle out, say, 150 yards in front of the road block where one man examines the traffic while another covers the examinee with his rifle. Then, should shots be fired, the main body of the guard is not taken by surprise.

TREES

Large trees felled across roads make good obstacles, but are very difficult to move quickly should our own vehicles wish to use the road. Because of this, think a long time before dropping a tree across the road. Bushy trees make good hiding-places for look-outs or fire bombers.

CAMOUFLAGE

Be most particular about camouflage; your life may depend on it. Do not allow tracks to be made near your posts, and when you camouflage a place so that the Boche cannot spot it, be sure to put something he *can* spot. This has a double use: not only will he waste ammunition on it, but as soon as he sees it (if it is not *too* obvious) he will **stop looking for the position you are trying to hide!**

By the way, the old Hun does not shoot with wonderful accuracy, so put your "distraction" a safe distance away from the real post.

BLUFF

In fighting the invader you should bluff like blazes. For example, suppose you have to block four streets in a desperate hurry, with visitors expected any moment. While your men are busy blocking the first street send two or three men to get carpets and clothes lines out of houses nearby and sling them across the streets so that the enemy cannot see beyond them. If you have not time to hang them vertically just lay them on the ground with bricks under them at intervals of a yard to make suspicious-looking humps.

No tank will dare to run over these without investigating them, and if you can fix a few A/T mines under one of them so much the better. Do not forget that Jerry will be sure to send someone on foot to lift up the carpet and see what is under, so detail men who can shoot to take advantage of this. It will be one Hun less, and you can put him under the carpet to make another suspicious hump.

Screens stop tanks from destroying your road block by shooting at it. They puzzle and annoy the enemy and often can be used to prevent the enemy seeing you move men across the street to counter-attack. If you are likely to be dive-bombed a dummy road block a hundred yards or more down the road may draw fire away from the defended one.

OTHER WEAPONS

Use every possible aid to defence you can scrounge up, from clothes lines to hoses throwing water or even live steam. If you have an electrician amongst your men he may be able to arrange something up to date in the way of entanglements.

Should the road block be likely to be rushed by refugees a trailer pump might be very useful.

FIGHTING PATROLS

Sometimes when the locality is suitable, a much stronger defence can be put up by fewer men if, instead of having guards at every block, just a few look-outs are posted and a strong fighting patrol, covering a number of road blocks, is kept ready to go into action in their defence immediately the look-outs signal danger. This obviates what so frequently happens when the enemy chooses one out of twenty road blocks for a determined attack which is borne by just a few of the defenders while the rest of them are stuck at other road blocks with nothing to do.

TRAPS

Anyone with an ingenious mind can devise all sorts of traps capable of doing everything from landing an approaching totalitarian on his nose to putting paid to a tank. The presence of a hidden trap gives confidence to the defence and a magnificent thrill when you see the enemy approaching it.

Try your hand at this: you may have a great flair!

ROUTINE

And now, in conclusion, I would like to point out that a lot of people have what may prove to be an entirely wrong idea about the length of time during which, if we have an alarm, road blocks will have to be manned.

It is possible that they may, in certain parts of the country, have to be defended day and night for weeks on end, and this will call for a properly organized routine.

The best way of making this clear is to show you specimens of ORDERS TO ROAD-BLOCK GUARD COMMANDER, and STANDING ORDERS FOR GUARDS ON ROAD BLOCKS.

If you study these you will at once see that the smooth running of a road-block guard calls for hard work and a really conscientious N.C.O. in charge.

Incidentally, it is very necessary to work out fair and equal spells of duty for all the men at the road block and post them up so that every man can see when he will be on duty as sentry, runner, etc., during the next forty-eight hours.

Posting them up has the added advantage that each man can see how much every other man is doing, and this cuts out the feeling that everyone seems to get after a time—the certainty that *he* is being worked harder than anyone else in the guard!

I attach great importance to these routine matters because when the testing time comes, and your guard has to FIGHT for the road block, possibly after days of suspense and waiting, you do not want them to be what the old soldier, with his love of alliteration, calls " bitched, b——d and bewildered " by loss of rest due to inefficient organization.

Your object should be to keep them FRESH AND FIGHTING FIT.

You can ensure this only by strict attention to routine details.

This has necessarily been a very sketchy outline of the siting and defence of road blocks, and there are aspects which I have, for various reasons, barely touched upon.

However, if I have succeeded in imparting to you my enthusiasm for this extraordinarily interesting subject, you will soon fill in the gaps and reason out the why and the wherefore for yourselves.

Appendix "A"

ORDERS TO ROAD-BLOCK GUARD COMMANDER

1. Duties

Immediately on arrival at the road block you will assign to each man his duties, men being detailed to:—

- (a) Close the gap when ordered.
- (b) Halt and examine traffic and pedestrians.
- (c) Defend the block with small-arms fire.
- (d) Act as bombers.
- (e) Keep a look-out, etc.

You will at once hold a rehearsal until you are satisfied that every man knows his position and his job.

2. Roster

A roster of duties will then be put up where every man can see it.

3. Points to Check

When taking over the road block you will make sure:—

- (a) That the STORES coincide with the inventory and are in good condition.
- (b) That necessary CROWBARS, LAMPS and TOOLS are on the site.
- (c) That everything necessary to close the road quickly is to hand, sockets cleared out and covers loosened.
- (d) That nothing obstructs LOOPHOLES, etc., and that no light of any kind can show through a loophole behind a man's head.
- (e) That fresh water is easily available.
- (f) That all BOMBS of all kinds are in perfect order and suitably placed.
- (g) That a half-filled sandbag is put into each loophole.
- (h) That SCREENS and CAMOUFLAGE are well arranged, suitably garnished and securely fixed.

(i) That all men are familiar with the RANGE CARD and can recognize objects shown.

(j) That SANITARY arrangements are clean, ample and known to all the men.

SHOULD ANYTHING BE LACKING, PLATOON HEADQUARTERS WILL BE NOTIFIED AT ONCE.

4. Equipment

You will daily inspect your men to ensure that all are CLEAN and properly dressed, that their ARMS AND EQUIPMENT are in perfect order, their AMMUNITION complete, RESPIRATORS in serviceable condition, and that all men have their FIELD DRESSINGS.

5. Orders

After inspection you will read to them the STANDING ORDERS, making sure that every man understands them.

Appendix "B"

STANDING ORDERS FOR GUARDS ON ROAD BLOCKS

It is the DUTY of every man to defend this road block against enemies of all kinds, whether on foot or in vehicles.

You will NOT, under any circumstances whatever, leave your post unless you are ordered to do so, or have been properly relieved.

Sentry Duty

When on sentry duty you will NOT leave your post unless properly relieved, remove any clothing or equipment, or talk to anyone except in carrying out your duties.

You will at all times watch and listen for

(a) Hostile persons approaching the road block or post.

(b) Air raids—parachutists—and gas.

Any unusual occurrence will at once be reported to the Guard Commander.

No unknown person (including officers) will be allowed to pass without satisfactory identification.

Opening Fire

Until a state of warfare actually develops, only the MINIMUM of force necessary to keep people away from the road block will be used. Should it be necessary to fire you must give CLEAR WARNING ("HALT or I FIRE!"), repeated twice.

If you are compelled to fire you will aim at enemy's legs, NOT over his head.

Bayonets

Bayonets will always be fixed, except during exercises.

Iron Rations

No man is allowed to consume iron rations without a special order to do so.

Night Traffic

Traffic will be halted at night by swinging a lamp.

Cleanliness

All men will take care to keep the road block and its surroundings clean and tidy.

JUST PUBLISHED

	s.	d.
"We Shall Fight in the Streets!" Guide to Street Fighting. By Capt. S. J. Cuthbert, Scots Guards. Illustrated (By Post, 2/9)	2	6

CONTENTS.—Ground—Defence—Attack—Use of Explosives—Arms and Equipment — Training — Exercises. Appendices — Protection Table — The Strengthening and Adaptation of a House for Defence—Syllabus for a Demonstration—Suppression of Civil Disturbances.

The Framing of an Exercise for the Home Guard. By Hanbury Pawle ... (By Post, 2/3) 2 0

CONTENTS.—Object—The Organization of the Exercise—The Lessons—Opening Narrative—The Scheme—Control of The Enemy—Umpiring—Road Blocks—Final Reflections.

Thoughts and Notes for Home Guard Commanders. By Hanbury Pawle ... (By Post, 1/8) 1 6

CONTENTS.—The Men of Britain—The Outlook Changes—The Invasion is Coming—Are the Home Guard ready To-day?—The Home Guard's Role—The Planning of Defence—The Details of Defence—Patrolling: The Reconnaissance Patrol—The Fighting Patrol—The Immediate Counter-Attack—Road Blocks—Action against Enemy Parachute Troops—To Conclude.

Notes on the Framing of Tactical Exercises. By Hanbury Pawle. With a Foreword by Field-Marshal Lord Ironside, G.C.B., C.M.G., D.S.O.... (By Post, 2/3) 2 0

CONTENTS.—Object—Imagination—Lessons—Opening Narrative—Narrative I—Advanced Guard—Attack—Defence—Rearguard—Concluding Remarks.

Aids to Weapon Training: Some Ideas on Improvization. By Lieut.-Colonel G. E. Thornton and Major H. de L. Waters, of the Small Arms School. Fully illustrated with diagrams and photographic plates ... (By Post, 2/3) 2 0

CONTENTS.—Rifle: Aiming Rests and Tripods ; Targets ; Marking Discs and Flags; Aiming Discs; Cover; Aim Correctors; Dummy; Record Books—Dummy Cartridges for all Makes of Weapons; How to Improvise These—The Bayonet: Standing Dummy; Guard Dummy; Training Stick; Assault Course—The 2-in. Mortar: Dummy Rounds; Aiming Rest; Cleaning Rods and Brushes; Smoke; The Sight—Anti-Tank Rifle: Dummies: $\frac{1}{30}$x Scale; Firing; Lead and Swing; Aim Corrector—Anti-Aircraft: Diagrams; Models—Aircraft Recognition: Features—Live Bombing and Mortar Ranges: Construction, Siting, etc.—Miniature Ranges: Construction; Battle Practice Targets—Field Firing: Targets; Communication—Booby Traps.

Theory of Rifle Fire. Fully illustrated with diagrams (Post, 1/8) 1 6

A concise manual of practical application, including details of trajectory, beaten zone, speed and penetration, and other useful information.

Accurate Shooting in War. By Major T. S. Smith (winner of H.M. The King's Prize, Bisley, 1939, and "The Grand Aggregate," Bisley, 1930). A commonsense approach to this aspect of Home Guard Training. Fully illustrated with photographic plates and line drawings ... (By Post, 1/8) 1 6

CONTENTS.—Extract from Western Command Home Guard Orders, Wednesday, 27th August, 1941—Preliminary Remarks—The Elements of Shooting—The Expert—The Marksman—Grouping—Zero—Preparation of the Barrel and Chamber—When to Shoot and at What Distance—The Hold—Firing Positions—The Bayonet—Aiming—Trigger Pressing—Follow Through—Immediate After Firing—Wind—Rain—Safety Precautions—Cleaning After Firing—Cleaning Generally—Oil—Muscle Exercises for Correct Holding of a Rifle—Aids to Shooting and Instruction—On the Open Range—The Butts—Marking in the Butts.

Combat without Weapons. Fully illustrated with 62 photographic plates. A simple textbook on this important phase of training ... (By post, 1/8) 1 6

Bloody Bayonets: A Complete Guide to Bayonet Fighting. By Squadron Leader R. A. Lidstone, R.A.F.V.R. Fully illustrated (By post, 2/3) 2 0

CONTENTS—The Two Weapons—Dress—Training Stick—Wall Pad—The Guard—The Target—Hits—Attack—Defence—The Beat—Throw Point, etc.—Close-up Fighting—The Butt—Unarmed Defence—Rules and Conventions of Bayonet Fighting—Pool System—Individual Competitions—Team Matches—Scoring.

Obtainable from all booksellers or direct from the publishers

GALE & POLDEN LTD. ALDERSHOT

A NEW SERIES OF TRAINING BOOKS
By COLONEL G. A. WADE, M.C.
(Author of "Defence of Bloodford Village.")

	s.	d.
House-to-House Fighting. Fully illustrated in colour (By Post, 1/8)	1	6

CONTENTS.—Objectives—Surprise—Covering Fire—Observation—Attack from Roofs—Attack through Cocklofts—Attack through Walls—Attacking Houses—Reserves—Smoke—Crossing Streets—Tackling Barricades—Defence of Houses—Cellars—Booby Traps—Street Fighting Competitions—Tanks in Towns.

The Art of Prowling. Fully illustrated (By Post, 1/2) **1 0**

CONTENTS.—Air-borne Attack—New Problems—Need for Prowlers—Objects of Prowling—How should he move?—Cunning Examples—Capture—Search—Challenging—Suspects—Parachutist: Description; How to shoot—Double Patrols, Night or Fog—Approaching Suspects—Use of Nature.

The Fighting Patrol. Fully illustrated in colour (By Post, 1/8) **1 6**

CONTENTS.—Home Guard Defence—Types of Patrol: Standing Patrol; Reconnoitring Patrol; Fighting Patrol—Objects of Fighting Patrol—Definite Task—Strength—Equipment—Formation—Movement—Unexpected Action—Communications: Field Signals—General Observations.

Fighting Patrol Training. Fully illustrated in colour (By Post, 1/8) **1 6**

CONTENTS.—Training—Six Characteristics—Determination to Attack—Skill in handling Weapons—Ability to move properly—Instinctive Reaction to Attack—Synchronization—Confidence—Street Fighting—How to clear Houses—Fighting Patrol Competitions—Example of Fighting Patrol Exercise—Observations on another Exercise—A Well-planned Fighting Patrol Action—Two Final Hints.

Fighting Patrol Tactics. Fully illustrated in colour (By Post, 1/8) **1 6**

CONTENTS.—Points before Starting—Parachutists—The Attack—The Defence—Night Patrols—Object of Fighting Patrol—Nature on our Side—Trees—Earth—Lie of Land: What to look for—Observation; Deduction; Action—Indoor Training.

Defence of Villages and Small Towns. Fully illustrated with plates and diagrams. In colour (By Post, 1/8) **1 6**

CONTENTS.—Strategic Importance of Villages—What Kind of Attack?—Oppose Force with Force—Which Parts Vital to Defend?—Need for Reserve—Siting the Keeps—Description of Keeps—Road Blocks—The Fighting Patrols—Men and Weapons—Rounding off the Defence Scheme—Liaison—Block Landing Grounds—Barbed Wire—Communications—Tank Traps—Water in Defence—Shot-guns—Training—Chronological Defence in Depth.

Road Blocks. Fully illustrated with plates and diagrams (By Post, 1/8) **1 6**

CONTENTS.—Importance of Road Blocks—Site your Road Blocks for Defence—Good Sites for Road Blocks—Active Defence of Road Blocks—Specimen Defence Action—Road Blocks in Depth—Mistakes in siting Road Blocks—Halting Traffic at a Distance—Trees—Camouflage—Bluff—Traps—Routine—Orders to Road Block—Guard Commanders—Standing Orders for Guards on Road Blocks.

Factory Defence. Fully illustrated with diagrams in colours (By Post 1/8) **1 6**

CONTENTS.—Size, Shape, Lay-out—What Have We to Defend It Against?: Attack by Thousands; Sabotage by Individuals or Small Parties—Average Factory can certainly Defend Itself—Countering the Saboteur—Study Each Vital Part Separately—How Shall We Stop Him ?—Do not be Content with Passive Defence—Keep a Watch on the Vital Parts—Help the Guard in Every Way—Principles to be Observed by Watchmen—Defence against Attack in Force—Split Factory into Vital and Non-Vital Parts—All-round Defence—Strengthening and Provisioning : Fire-fighting Equipment, Sandbags, Wire—Alternative Positions: Mark Loopholes in readiness—Careful Study of Plan—Aggressive Defence—Kostinoff Brickworks—You will find Principles apply to Your Factory—Final Hints.

*Obtainable from all booksellers
or direct from the publishers*

GALE & POLDEN LTD. ALDERSHOT
also on sale at their showrooms

LONDON:
Ideal House, Argyll St.,
Oxford Circus, W.1

PORTSMOUTH:
Nelson House,
Edinburgh Road

Also from Royal Armouries Publishing

The Art of Prowling

It is extraordinary how reluctant the British soldier is to show cunning. We try to play the game of war as if it had rules for fair play like cricket and football.

If you want to make your spell of duty pass quickly, concentrate on prowling properly.

By Jove, look! There is a suspicious-looking man creeping under those bushes. It will be heaven help that rough chap if he makes a break!

The Art of Prowling showed recruits how to sneak up on the enemy without being seen, how to avoid attracting attention, and why they should never underestimate a German spy.

Will you be awarded the Good Prowler's Badge?

House to House Fighting

Do you know that house-to-house fighting is the finest sport on earth?

Do you know that is it just the sort of close-quarter scrapping we British excel in?

Do you know that once you get going you will *love* it?

Do you want to come with me down our street and play hell with some bloody Huns?

You do?

Right, we'll carry on!

Defence of Houses

·DEFENCE·
OF HOUSES
by COL. G. A. WADE, M.C.
Author of "The Defence of Bloodford Village" etc.

THE GALE & POLDEN
TRAINING SERIES

Price 1/6 net. by post 1/8

When the enemy invade us the most stubborn fighting will be in the built-up areas where their tanks will not be able to help them much.

Houses are found in infinite variety. Some are suited for defence, others are absolute death-traps.

Think: is it strong? Has it a cellar? Are its surrounding suitable? Is it capable of all-round defence?

Let me impress upon you once again: let your defence be active; go out and hit the enemy first; keep hitting him as he draws near to your defended house; and have your defences so good and so cunning, both inside and outside, that when he begins to attack it you can heave a sigh of relief and say, 'And now he's going to ask for it, and he *will* get it!'

Fire Control

Home Guard Training Series

FIRE CONTROL
by COL. G.A. WADE M.C.
Author of "The Defence of Bloodford Village" etc.

Price 1/6 net by post 1/8

How often do we hear commanders say they are practically defenceless without machine guns and anti-tank weapons?

Yet they have hundreds of men armed with the finest weapon of all – the rifle!

For general use there is nothing to take its place. Nothing so universally deadly; nothing to beat it in attack and defence.